B.L.O.G.

BREAKTHROUGH, LISTEN, & OBEY GOD

TO

MARRIAGE

B.L.O.G.

BREAKTHROUGH, LISTEN, & OBEY GOD

TO

MARRIAGE

By. Thomas and Candace Claiborn IV

"A LOVE STORY SERIES"
A DEVOTIONAL FOR COUPLES

FOREWORD BY: DR. LINDSAY MARSH
Author of "The Best Sex of My Life"

Order this book online at www.trafford.com
or email orders@trafford.com

Most Trafford titles are also available at major online book retailers.

Printed in Victoria, BC, Canada.

ISBN: 978-1-4269-2821-5 (sc)

*Our mission is to efficiently provide the world's finest, most comprehensive
book publishing service, enabling every author to experience success.
To find out how to publish your book, your way, and have it available
worldwide, visit us online at www.trafford.com*

Trafford rev. 4/05/2010

Trafford PUBLISHING® www.trafford.com

North America & international
toll-free: 1 888 232 4444 (USA & Canada)
phone: 250 383 6864 ♦ fax: 812 355 4082

This book is dedicated to Jesus Christ the author and perfecter of our faith. Also, to the many great examples of healthy, productive, and authentic marriages that we have been blessed with the privilege of witnessing.

B.L.O.G. to MARRIAGE

Is to every individual interested in taking the first steps towards building a successful, strong, and fruitful marriage.

ACKNOWLEDGEMENTS

We are sincerely appreciative to all of those who have supported us through our journey of courtship and who continue to stand by us in marriage.

Thank you to our parents, grandparents, siblings, friends, Grace Covenant Church family, and mentors. You have all truly been an inspiration to us and have taught us many things along the way both about relationships and about ourselves as individuals. Your prayers, finances, and emotional support have truly been a blessing.

Thank you for your listening ears, giving hands, and encouraging lips. We pray that God will continue to draw us closer together as we each draw closer to Him. May God bless you and return to you one hundred-fold that which you have poured into our lives.

We would like to give special thanks to Dr. Lindsay Marsh, Pastor Darryl and JoAnn Morrison, Janel Dear, and Tanyell and Jabulani Cole of Xclusively yourZ photo memories, for their contributions to the creation of this book, including the forward, backward, introduction, and authors' photo.

Lastly, thank you to all of our blog followers for your encouragement, feedback, and accountability throughout our journey to marriage.

We look forward to having the privilege of seeing the great things God has in store for each and every one of you.

Contents

FOREWORD
BY DR. LINDSAY MARSH

I have had the delightful experience of watching Thomas and Candace Claiborn in the dating and courtship seasons of their relationship. In fact, Candace lived with me during her senior year at George Washington University. She often referred to nuggets I shared in my book, "The Best Sex of My Life: a guide to Purity", how it correlated to their own dating practices and ways they were protecting one another in courtship. Thomas read the book for himself and wrote a blog about it observing, inspiring and befriending this couple has been indelibly joyous for me!

"B.L.O.G. to Marriage" possesses practical advice for a season of pure courtship and the days leading to holy matrimony. How do you handle the emotions? How do you handle the hormones? How do you handle the physical attraction while maintaining a pure heart before the Lord? Tommy and Candace will show you how, in this courtship devotional. Candace and Tommy were the first couple to be married, after having both been Worth The Wait Revolution models and partners with our ministry. It was so humbling to see the hand of the Lord on their wedding, families and finances. It is obvious that even in this season, when you first seek the kingdom of God and His righteousness, all these things will be added unto you. (Matthew 6:33) Let Candace and Tommy show you how to seek kingdom things and put God first, in the season of your courtship and engagement. The rewards will be limitless.

Lindsay S. Marsh, MD

President

Worth The Wait Revolution, Inc

MARRIAGE

Marriage: A lifelong Covenant between a male and female that produces much fruit.

The First Marriage: Jesus Christ (Husband) and the Church (his Bride)

Man's Tangible Expression of Marriage: Male (Husband) and A Female (his Bride)

"A LOVE STORY"

Thomas and Candace met on January 27, 2007 on the campus of Howard University; she recognized him from the church she had recently joined, Grace Covenant Church, in DC. Two weeks later he "friended" her on Facebook and in the following weeks they went on their first date. A month later their courtship began.

After a year and a half of courting, Thomas proposed to Candace in Jamaica after her parent's 25th wedding anniversary celebration. One year later on July 18, 2009, they wed in Atlanta, GA.

They honeymooned in the Dominican Republic and are now fulfilling Their "Love Story" and living in Alexandria, VA. Attending Grace Covenant Church DC apart of the Every Nation Family....

ABOUT US:

Hi!! We are a recently married couple (July 18th, 2009) and a part of the "WORTH THE WAIT" Revolution Family. On our journey towards marriage we started a blog of encouragement to share with others that "Wait" doesn't necessarily mean FOREVER!!! Based off of those blogs we have now turned them into a book that shares our thoughts, failures, struggles, and breakthroughs that we battled on our journey to marriage. Follow us as we follow Christ!!!

THOMAS CLAIBORN IV

Thomas Claiborn IV was born in Silver Spring, MD and raised in Pittsburgh, PA. He grew up in Penn Hills, a suburb of Pittsburgh. Thomas attended Mt. Olive Baptist Church in Rankin, PA where he gave his life to Lord in October 2001. When Thomas graduated from High School he attended Howard University where he got connected with Grace Covenant Church in Washington, DC where he still serves to this day. Grace Covenant is a relationship building church that focuses on individuals being and making disciples.

CANDACE CLAIBORN

Candace Sheree Claiborn was born in Bronx, NY and moved to the suburb of Kennesaw, GA at the age of 9. She gave her life to Christ at 12 yrs old but it wasn't until joining Word Up Bible Study, lead by Dr. Lindsay Marsh, during her junior year of college at The George Washington University in Washington, D.C. that she got serious about serving the Lord. In fall of 2006 she became a member of Grace Covenant Church, and has been growing and serving there for the past three years.

INTRO

As my friend, pastor, and one who has discipled me, Darryl Morrison, always says, and I feel will always be true, "You Haven't Arrived". I believe no matter where we are in life we have the capacity to become better and we're called to BREAKTHROUGH barriers, LISTEN and OBEY GOD. We are not yet what God wants us to become.

Here in America it is very easy to say that we are Christians and we Love God; but the real question is: Do our actions correspond with what we say? How we behave in relationships is one tangible way to really show if we Love God or not. This is a book about God's standards not ours. By which Candace and I have fallen way below in our relationship and in previous relationships. Thank goodness for Jesus Christ who cleanses us from those actions and gives us the power (Holy Spirit) to turn around and stand up for God's standards. At our church we like to call it HOLDING THE LINE!

Thomas

Friday, August 29, 2008

Question?

Candace and I had already established that we were **"Worth the Wait"** to ourselves before we met. But when we found the person whom we thought Christ actually had us waiting for; waiting got just a little bit harder.

Our Vision for this ~~blog~~ now book was to be a sense of encouragement to others who are also waiting, and for us to testify that God is faithful. Also, we wanted to help to share Practical Wisdom on ways to stay out of compromising situations; and more importantly help individuals overcome struggles, breakthrough strongholds so that they may truly grow towards Christ, and have success in living a sexual pure lifestyle and other areas as well...Please get connected to God and with other individuals that follow Christ to hold you accountable. I would like to Spark this off by asking a simple question...

"What do you look forward to gain out of this ~~Blog~~/ Book"? Ideas, Thoughts and Concerns...Write them down for yourself...

~Tommy

Posted by Candace and Tommy at <u>5:58 AM</u>

Write on your Heart: *I Thessalonians 4:3-8*

_____

_____

_____

_____

_____

_____

_____

_____

_____

_____

_____

_____

_____

_____

_____

_____

_____

_____

_____

_____

_____

_____

Friday, September 5, 2008

<u>The X-Factor</u>

Over this past Holiday Weekend Candace and I got asked a question about our Boundaries. Basically the question was "How X-TREME are they?" And "Why?" Throughout our relationship we have gotten crazy type advice on setting boundaries, some we have taken some we have ignored. Examples being not Hugging, Kissing or even holding hands. Others, not being together one-on-one, having curfews, and plenty more. Boundaries are important and setting X-TREME boundaries are really great to keep you from falling into temptation. A prime example of this is shown by Adam& Eve. If you read Genesis closely you can see the X-TREME boundary that they had in place. Gods command to Adam was to simply not eat from the Tree of The Knowledge of Good and Evil (Gen2:17). But later, (Gen 3:3) Eve insisted to the serpent that they couldn't even touch the tree or else they would surely die (I'd say an X-TREME boundary). They took their Boundary one step further; I'm pretty sure if they would have stayed true to their X-TREME boundary and not have even touched the tree they wouldn't have had a problem with not eating the fruit. While all boundaries are different for all relationships, the questions really are "Do you Set X-TREME boundaries?" "Are they clearly stated?" and "Do you hold true to them?" Or can any smooth talking serpent come up to you and knock over your boundaries?

~Tommy

Posted by Candace and Tommy at <u>8:50 AM</u>

-Great blog!!! Important blog for all those who are Worth the Wait!!! I will be back to comment more :-)

- Great post. I never noticed that Tree of Knowledge boundary before. Strong stuff!

-Good stuff!!!

Write on your Heart:
*Genesis 2:15-17
*Genesis 3:3

Monday, September 15, 2008

<u>"Red Light, Green Light, 123"</u>

I'm so annoyed right now because the blog I just typed for ya'll is completely gone, Word shut down and took with it my blog, so now I'm starting from scratch. I hope it's as good as the last. Lol

So I was talking about how Tommy and I made the decision not to kiss (like on the lips) until our wedding day. Some may think it's extreme or just plain silly, but for us it's a choice we made a year and eight months ago because we know ourselves and we understand the difference between something being "permissible and beneficial" (1corinthians 6:12)

I mean, for some people kissing is like an alternative hug and for others it's the closest thing to having sex. For me I know kissing is just going to leave me wanting more and more and more, and ...well you get the point. Lol As said by minister Lindsay Marsh, "we weren't created to have to stop," and I am a true believer of that...let's finish what we started you know what I mean.

Anyway, to be honest Tommy is the first person I have ever made such a commitment with, and it wasn't easy making the decision, nor is it easy keeping it. I mean, for the most part it's been cool, but I know I'm not the only one that gets "physically frustrated" sometimes and simply wants to have sex. And ladies and gentlemen, being engaged makes it no easier. The idea of being married in only 10 months and knowing that you'll be able to have all the sex , and do all the kissing you want, really messes a sistah's mind up. I mean, Wow!

Just the idea of being able to make love with the person you plan on spending the rest of your life with, and being able to then get up and joyfully go to church or say a quick prayer about how great the sex was, completely blows my mind.

And ladies and gents, that's partly what keeps me committed, not to mention the public commitment we have made. And don't get me wrong, it's not about showing others how strong or pure we can be, but it's really about knowing and following God's voice that leads you as an individual. Not everyone has felt that tug on their heart to make such a commitment, so I'm not here to tell you how to make that decision. But I am here as a human being that is working by God's grace with my fiancé' to stay true to a major commitment.

When it really boils down to it, I have to be real with myself and I have to analyze the set up of the battle. Is it just about Tommy and I or is it bigger than us? How will this choice to break this commitment affect even bigger commitments in our marriage? And the list goes on.

If I'm willing to let this commitment go by the way side all for a quick tease that I know can't really satisfy me, than will I allow just a little online porn in our home, or even just a casual lunch date with a co-worker….

So instead of practicing how to be unfaithful, Tommy and I chose to practice faithfulness to one another and to Christ.

So when times get rough and your contemplating just a little this…a little that…really challenge yourself to look past the moment and look into your future. Is it all about you or is there an even bigger picture that's being clouded by that strong desire to be sexually and emotionally satisfied.

And just little tip: if you find yourself second guessing or thinking really hard on something, you should probably stick to your guns and not do whatever you're thinking about doing.

It's kind of like driving: some things are really obvious like Don't go through the RED light, Definitely go through the GREEN light,…but when you get to a YELLOW light it gets a little sticky for some; if you're like me you tend to hesitate on going through or deciding to stop. But all in all you know you should just stop, and the whole 2 seconds that you're trying to make the light before it turns RED, you're praying and hoping to God there wasn't a cop there or at least that the flash you just saw in your rear view mirror wasn't the remains of a photo of your license plate. Lol

So I do what I know is best for me: I say what I'm feeling out loud, I remind myself why I'm keeping to my commitment, and I try to move out of the circumstance that is making me want to take the risk and go through that yellow light.

We have to step our game up; we aren't 8 and 9 years old anymore and "red light, green light 123" isn't something we do to past time by, it's our future!

~ Candace

Posted by Candace and Tommy at <u>5:50 AM</u>

-Great blog!!!! I loved the Red, Green, and Yellow Light analogy! Made things really clear. I think all in all, people tend to focus on all that we can't do rather than what we should be doing to enhance ourselves. So, I appreciate you stating that this commitment to God is in turn preparing the both of you to stay committed to one another when you do get married. I mean....if you can't keep a promise to the one that gave His life for you...how much more an ordinary human being?

Wow, I guess I never really thought about the commitment aspect you talked about. Hmmmmm...Keeping a commitment now and its impact on later commitments is so key. I think you brought up some really great keys that definitely ministered to me.

-I'm so proud of you guys.

-I'm loving this Blog. It's great to see couples committing to each other in such a way. My Gentleman friend and I are also waiting for each other. My traffic light situation only happens with whom I consider to be the one and I know what that is like to be given the Green light then had to get to that yellow light and finally say to yourself STOP. It's basically painful and frustrating. Personally I feel like it's more difficult for me. My GF has no problem. I'm sure he gets more frustrated at times but that time at the yellow light just kills me. Ok I'm getting a little long winded here. Keep the blogs coming.

Write on Your Heart: *1 Corinthians 6:12*

Tuesday, September 23, 2008

<u>The "1"</u>

What Your Engaged? Are you sure? Wait, How old are you? There are so many females why settle for one? Why? Ahhh that's great! Good luck with that…Wait, Why again?? That's Cool!! .. Well how do you know you've found "The One "???

All typical conversations I go through now being engaged. No matter who or wherever I'm conversing with someone if the subject that I'm engaged comes up it usually leads down the path of these responses. Here and Now, I will concentrate on the last question which seems to come up the most. How do you know you've found "The ONE". I 'm always tempted to answer the question with "I don't I'm just going to try my LUCK and see how it goes ". Although being the closest thing to the TRUTH that answer always seems as if it would draw an entertaining response back, even though that is the reality that most people asking that question are living in as they speak. The answer most people are content with is "You Just Know" so that's usually what I give them but the Real answer goes much deeper than that. One thing Candace and I established early in our relationship was that we were each other's # 2's with Jesus being each of our # 1 (Not a bad person to come in second place to.) Once, we noticed in each other that we both had already found "THE ONE" it was very easy for us to slide into our vacant # 2 spots. The Cool thing about Jesus being in your #1 spot is that there is no higher standard that your #2 can ask of you that isn't already required of you. So if you find someone that is fully submitted to that #1 spot it's very easy to know if you've found "The One " or not …"You just Know"!!!!… In my eyes LUCK is when Preparation meets Opportunity… L.U.C.K. –   Laboring Under Correct Knowledge

My questions: Who are you preparing for, someone who knows "THE ONE" or someone you want to be "THE ONE"???? Who are you trying your LUCK on?? WRITE IT DOWN FOR YOURSELF!!

~ Tommy

Write on your Heart: *Matthew 6:33*

_____

_____

_____

_____

_____

_____

_____

_____

_____

_____

_____

_____

_____

_____

_____

_____

_____

_____

_____

Sunday, October 26, 2008

"TONE DEAF"???

First and Foremost, we would like to apologize for our hiatus, but marriage preparation and wedding planning has taken rank over the blog for the past couple of weeks. Next, we would like to thank you all for the encouraging emails, Facebook notes, and posts. It is uplifting for Candace and me to know that God is using this blog to advance His kingdom. I would also like to reiterate how this blog is open for discussion; our hearts behind this blog is not only to help others trying to advance their relationship with Christ, but to grow within ourselves as well. Finally, I would like to say we will be more consistent from here on out with a weekly blog post where Candace and I will be alternating. PLEASE FEEL FREE TO HOLD US ACCOUNTABLE!!!

So for this Week I would really just like to share what Christ has been working on in me lately. I'm really excited about marriage not just for the Fringe benefits, but really to see the next level that Christ has called me to be at. Women have to go from submitting to God to submitting to an imperfect human (Wish Candace Good-Luck with that) While Men must learn how to treat their wives with the Compassion, Kindness, and Grace that Christ treats the Church with and for me I can already tell this will be a battle. Now, one thing that the Married Men that I have pouring into my life have been teaching me is how God places your mate with you to pull out qualities in you that you could not have pulled out of yourself by yourself. In other words, your spouse will have the ability to point out your strengths and weaknesses in places you can't see them. Therefore, in our relationship one of the weakness that Candace has pointed out in me is my "Tone" Over and Over again she has restated to me " Its not what you say, Its How you say it" and I have to almost always re frame my statement to make sure it is expressed out of Love not anger.

I write all this to ask …"How do we interpret Gods "Tone"? Or a better question is, "How do we misinterpret it? When I misinterpret Gods heart and "Tone" behind the true design for Sex it kind of makes me feel like I'm missing out on something, but in reality the only thing I'm missing out on is God's Loving heart and "Tone". When I flip God's "Tone" from a reprimanding Father that Screams, "NO YOU CANT HAVE SEX," to a Loving Father's voice that simple states, "You can have it, but just not Yet," it makes it more simple for me to not go away thinking, "Ahh Man I can't do that!!" …But Understanding ohh he's trying to protect me from Heartache, losing friendships, and trying to bless me with the ability to communicate with my future spouse so we don't rely on Sex for our marriage to work.

"Sex is a by product of marriage, marriage is not a by product of Sex" So while I have to reassure Candace Over and Over again what I say is out of Love no matter what my "Tone," we can be fully certain that Everything Christ says is out of LOVE!! How do you interpret Christ "Tone" to you?

~Tommy

Posted by Candace and Tommy at 9:17 PM

-Wow! First off I would like to say I think that is so cool that you guys have a blog together. It shows you are really committed to not only each other, but serving everyone, who needs advice, encouragement and stuff, and it shows your commitment to Christ and his principles. I support this movement because waiting isn't forever. Being that I don't have a girlfriend right now, I'm learning how to love my future wife. It's hard sometimes because you can't see her, but that's where the faith comes in! And although I love her so much already, expressing my feelings and stuff can be so hard. It's frustrating sometimes, lol. But I'm just happy that the Lord is working on me in that area of my life. So it's interesting you call this article tone deaf, because sometimes I feel like I am. But I believe that's why God equips you with the necessary tools to be successful. So that is my blog, wish the best blessings to you guys!

-<u>Candace</u> said...Wow; it's encouraging to know that you are being blessed by our stories. I wish you the best as you wait on the Lord as it pertains to your wife. Long before I ever had thoughts of Tommy or even knew he would be my husband, I prayed for him daily. I encourage you to even keep a journal of your thoughts of her, your prayers and love for her, so that when you do finally find your missing rib, she can always be reminded of how much you love her. And similar to what God says about us, " You saw me before I was born...Every moment was laid out before a single day had passed...How precious are your thoughts about me, O God. They cannot be numbered!" (Psalm 139:16, 17)

As marriage is the mirror of Christ and the Church, I think you're off to a great start by loving your wife even before seeing her, just as God loved us and knew us before we were even born.

God Bless!!!

-I am glad you all are BACK! Yes...I do forgive you for your absence and look forward to some exciting blogs!

-WOW, WOW, WOW! I think it's really the Lord's hand that led me here! My Fiancé and I have recently turned our hearts toward Christ and are on a "worth the wait" mission too! It's really refreshing to know there are more young people out there of like minds. I am thrilled actually. Everything I have read so far on your blog is confirming EVERYTHING that the Lord has been revealing to us over the past few months since we've decided to take this new step. There's so much more I could say but I hope to have the opportunity to share more with you both soon. In the meantime: keep up the encouraging and refreshing demonstration of Christ in your union and may God Bless you both continually!

Kind Regards.

Write on your Heart: *Ephesians 5:22-33*

_____

_____

_____

_____

_____

_____

_____

_____

_____

_____

_____

_____

_____

_____

_____

_____

_____

_____

_____

_____

Monday, November 3, 2008

<u>What happens when the things you thought were dead, keep coming up alive in your relationship?</u>

Wow, I cannot even begin to tell you how much your past can really challenge your present and future relationships. There is so much in my past that I thought I had really dealt with, until Tommy and I began to dig deep into the conflict and communication break downs between us. We've all heard it before that "women are more emotional than men and that we carry all our emotional baggage around" and inadvertently smacking every new relationship in the face, walking around saying, "oh I'm sorry, ooh didn't mean to do that…." until the person finally walks away thinking to themselves, "Whoa…I'm so tired of getting smacked in the face and hearing all these apologies, yet still getting hit for no APPARENT reason (Apparent being the key word).

The baggage that I have wasn't always so visible; I think for some of us (if I can speak for the women) our "baggage" is sometimes just put in a new or different bag like a wristlet or a wallet. It gets so clouded and cluttered by the things that make us feel good (like the lip gloss, and makeup) that you don't even realize it's in there. It's kind of like your driver's license. I hardly every even think to check that it's in my purse; when I go into my bag it's not ever to get my license, it's to get some lip gloss or body spray, or gum. If you think about it, most of the times you're asked to show your ID, it's to verify or prove something (and for me an uncomfortable feeling); like being pulled over for speeding, or trying to buy alcohol or get into a club and you're under age. In all of those instances just the idea of having to pull out your ID makes you a little nervous and that after taking it out the first thing you want to do is to put it right back in your purse, and the last thing you want is for you to be denied access because your license "baggage" has been denied.

In my present circumstance, my baggage from previous relationships and my feelings of insecurity and fear, have been tucked away in a small/unused compartment of my purse (life and heart), and now that I have iron (Tommy) trying to sharpen iron (me), I'm being forced to really dig deep and verify some things in my heart: why I do certain things, and why I think a certain way. And as sharp as that iron is sometimes, and as quickly as I sometimes just want to put my baggage away, I have to really attack the issues at heart and let God do the true renovation and beautification that's required for me to live freely. Don't just get your issues a new bag to sit in, rather un -zip the bag, pour it all out on a table (it doesn't have to be all at once) , and honestly share the issues so that you can be well- sharpened; ready to cut through even the hardest things in life.

~ Candace

Posted by Candace and Tommy at <u>2:36 PM</u>

-So very true! I agree that it's those small things, small compartments as you say that can ultimately cause the rifts of divisiveness and this is all relevant for any covenant relationship.

-This makes me think of my daily interactions with those I am connected to in relationship. My unwillingness or even ignorance to acknowledge those small things which may hinder my relationships are a constant, daily reminder of the conditions that I place on love. Yet, how blessed I am to walk in relationship those is my life!

-This is so true, Candace! And while it's not fun "unzipping" the bag, it is very much needed. Thank God Tommy is a man of God who realizes that he is to help you in the process! This makes me think back on the time when Rev. Tony Lee came to Word Up! And he was talking about how we're at such a key point in our lives and now is the time to work on issues that we may have and get closure so that we don't carry that baggage with us as we get older.

Thomas & Candace Claiborn IV

Write on your Heart: Luke 6:46-49

22

Monday, November 10, 2008

<u>His-story… Makes History!</u>

Over this past week I've seen 50 cent Newspaper's "Worth" go off the charts! So I asked myself: Why is that? For some people it was the historical aspect, others wanted to be able to show their children what they were apart of, and others got the papers because they thought it would be "Worth" a lot of something long down the road. I mean these papers are already going for $200 plus on E-Bay, which I think is pretty tight. But if we can imagine how a newspaper that a day before November 5th or a day after is only "Worth" Picking up a dogs poop, can be enhanced by a historical life changing event imagine how much a persons self "Worth" can be enhanced when it is identified with Christ, and "THE HISTORICAL LIFE CHANGING EVENT".

Can we imagine the historical aspect of living the way Christ has called us to live? Can we imagine passing down the Legacy of Sexual Purity to our children, and showing them the way a true marriage is to be displayed? Can we imagine sharing with people not what they think they will be "Worth" down the road but what Christ actually promises we are "Worth" today? I personally didn't get this newspaper that could be "Worth" so much in the future, and has so much historical significance, but my Bride to be (Candace) did, so luckily I didn't miss-out on this historical opportunity but I'm pretty sure I would have been fine without my newspaper. On the contrary, one opportunity I refuse to miss-out on is being apart of "His-story" and living my life to have a lasting impact on "History". My questions are who are you letting define your "Worth"? Is it Christ? Or some other outside forces?

~ Tommy

Posted by Candace and Tommy at <u>7:13 PM</u>

-Man Tommy,

This was really good! I liked how you drew a link to the 'historical newspaper' and how its worth went up due to the fact that Obama made history. I was one of those many standing in a couple of lines to get this "valuable" piece of history. Now imagine if people could realize the significance of adding the value of Christ to their live. The worth He would add to them. This made me think about the legacy I am building in my walk with Christ and what value I will be able to pass down generations ahead. GREAT STUFF!!!

Write on your Heart: John 15:1-17

_____

_____

_____

_____

_____

_____

_____

_____

_____

_____

_____

_____

_____

_____

_____

_____

_____

_____

_____

_____

Tuesday, November 18, 2008

<u>Godly Counsel is Paramount!!</u>

Wow, I cannot begin to tell you how important it is to truly and proactively seek Godly counsel. Throughout our relationship Tommy and I have made a great effort to build relationship with leaders in the body of Christ that will be able and available to guide us through this new experience of engagement and future marriage. Whether it was reading books or just spending time with mentors from church, we knew that we needed support and additional perspectives in order to make this thing work.

And after experiencing our first "official" pre-marital counseling with a couple from our church, I am truly blown at the fact that people can really commit to a marriage without ever going through any kind of counseling or even a relationship building with Christ.

God is truly at the center of marriage and if you don't have His heart about it, then you might as well sign the pre-nup and hang on for the ride that's a downward ending slope; that's after you tried to keep it exciting with sex and all.

This thing called marriage is NO Joke!!! Our meeting with the counselors really brought to light the reality of marriage and the joys and pains that will inevitably come along with it. I've heard it time and time again how marriage is real work, but I'm putting on my Timberlands and tightening my tool belt because it's going to take some serious submission and elbow grease for two imperfect people to exemplify God's perfect union and display of His relationship with us as His children.

I'm realizing more and more each day how paramount it is for me to be on my A-game in order to contribute to our future marriage. I know I can't get there alone so I'm glad we have Godly counsel to help us along the way.

~ Candace.

Write on your Heart: Proverbs 15:22

_____

_____

_____

_____

_____

_____

_____

_____

_____

_____

_____

_____

_____

_____

_____

_____

_____

_____

_____

_____

Tuesday, November 25, 2008

<u>Vision</u>

Over the past week Candace and I mapped out a vision for our marriage and I also made a list of goals for myself as well. I already have July 18th 2059 marked on my calendar because that will be the day we celebrate our 50th yr wedding anniversary. Candace is really good at mapping out her vision on paper while for me this is my first time but I would encourage everyone to do so. The word of God says: write down your vision on a tablet and make it plain so others may run with it. Therefore, with that being said we wanted to make our vision very simple and suitable for our children's, children's, children to be able to take it and run with it. We want to clearly make the declaration that all generational curses end with us at least any that we're capable of ending. A declaration like that can only be accomplished by having a God ordained vision. The Pastors at our church put a lot of emphasis on passing the baton to the next generation like in a track meet, and we don't want our next generation to have to start with the baton out of the starting blocks but we want them to already be running and for it to be a simple exchange from us to them so they can take it and run with it. Writing out a vision doesn't just give us a clear understanding of what we want out of life, but better yet it gives us a very clear description of what we don't want out of life. So whether if you're single or in a relationship you should map out a vision for qualities that you are looking for in a mate, or out of a relationship, and for your future. "Faith is being sure of what you hope for and certain of what

you do not see." What don't you see that you are hoping for??
WRITE IT DOWN FOR YOURSELF!

~ Tommy

Write on your Heart: *Hebrews: 11:1*

Monday, December 1, 2008

"Truth"

Who is the judge?
The judge is God.
Why is he God?
Because he decides who wins or loses. Not my opponent.
Who is your opponent?
He does not exist.
Why does he not exist?
Because he is a mere dissenting voice of the truth I speak!"
"The Great Debaters"

My dad has this saying that has stuck with me for years; he says, "Speak the truth, speak it ever, call it what you will. He who hides the wrong he does, does the wrong thing still."

I gather from this quote that whether you speak it or not, the truth still exists.

My auntie Regna has taught me that if you want to be able to distinguish the truth from a lie, you study the real thing, so that the counterfeit will be easy to spot. Studying the truth takes a lot of commitment and along with it sometimes comes hurt feelings and shame.

There's something about hearing the truth that can be really difficult. I don't know about you but hearing the truth about my faults and areas of much needed growth is pretty painful. I mean, deep down inside whether verbalized or not, you already know what you would like to work on about yourself! But actually hearing it is even more real. But ladies and gentlemen at the end of the day it's all about the work that **God** is doing in you and it doesn't matter the person He chooses to speak through.

But for me I have been blessed to have Tommy as God's truth -speaking mouth piece. And oooh boy his truth is real. We've shared with you before about the importance of tone, but even when the truth is spoken in love, the way he does so well, the bottom line is it's still the truth! I'm learning that true love tells the truth and true love listens to the truth. After all as my soon to be husband, who better than to tell me the truth despite the temporary pain I may feel. As my husband he will be the example of Christ and I will be the example of the church (Ephesians 5:25) and the Word of God says that Christ is, "...the way, the **truth**, and the life..." (John 14:5) To accompany Christ as the truth, 1John 5:16 says that, "God is love, and all who live in love live in God, and God lives in them... (verse 17) and as we live in God, our love grows more perfect."

So what am I saying? I'm saying that no matter how badly the truth sometimes hurts, as Tommy lives in God and as we prepare to be ambassadors for God's design for marriage (a mirror image of His relationship with us the church), then the truth he speaks helps to grow our love for God and one another more perfect!

So don't get upset or frustrated with the person that tells you the truth; after all they are not your opponent, your opponent does not exist! They are just the mouth-piece chosen by God, who is the judge.

~Candace

Posted by Candace and Tommy at <u>1:19 PM</u>

-It's not that we discount the devil's existence. Scripture (and life) tells us that he does. However, he doesn't speak truth. The devil IS a "dissenting voice of the truth I speak."

-At times I feel that we give the devil too much place. Is he real? Yes. Does he mess stuff up? Yes? But more times than not...it is because we let him.

Write on your Heart: *John 14:5*

_____

_____

_____

_____

_____

_____

_____

_____

_____

_____

_____

_____

_____

_____

_____

_____

_____

_____

_____

Tuesday, December 9, 2008

<u>Max-Out!!</u>

A few weeks ago I read Dr. Lindsay Marsh's Book "Best Sex of My Life" a Guide to Sexual Purity. I thought the book was great it gives great practical knowledge for keys to living a sexually pure life. As for me, before I had this crazy idea that sexual purity ended once you got married; I had this insane mindset that once you got married you could have all the sex that you wanted, so I just thought it made sense that sexual purity was over once the wedding bands went on the fingers. On the contrary, I learned that Sexual purity does not have an expiration date but it is a lifestyle. Things that can have an effect on us outside of marriage if not dealt with can have a huge effect on the relationship after marriage. Examples being the music we listen to, masturbation, pornography, and anything we allow our eyes to see or our ears to hear that doesn't glorify God. I heard someone say once, that the devil does whatever possible to make you have sex before marriage and whatever possible to prevent you from having sex after marriage. With that being said I take it upon myself to make sure I don't give the devil any opportunity to ruin the "Best Sex of my Life". How do I try to do this? By getting a clear distinct definition of what Sex actually is created for and that definition can only be given by its creator. The Definition: SEX- is designed to be shared between a Male and a Female after they have made a Covenant with one another. If we accept anything other than that, we would be cutting ourselves short and we would not reach our maximum potential of enjoyment. I want to reach my max in life How about you?

~ Tommy

Posted by Candace and Tommy at <u>5:48 PM</u>

Write on your Heart: *I Corinthians 9:24-27*

Tuesday, December 16, 2008

<u>Stir It Up!</u>

Earlier in the week I was feeling really bored with my life; I felt like, "wow, I do the same thing day in- day out… work, church, home…time with Tommy…time with friends…and quickly I return back to work." I started comparing my life to that of some people on facebook; some folks appeared to being having so much fun, their lives looked so interesting. Bottom line, I was being deceived by the enemy that my life somehow was boring because everything I do almost always rounds back to church and my relationship building with Tommy.

I was feeling really discouraged, but after spending some time in the Bible reading up on who God says I am and soaking in some great advice from an awesome friend of mine, Dr. Lindsay Marsh, my eyes were opened and I realized that, "No! My life is not boring, and Yes! Praise God it's centered on the things it is centered around! I am who I am because that's who God has called me to be! I am in the position I am in because that's the place God has for me at this divine moment in my life…and how dare I even entertain the destructive ideas of Satan that something is somehow wrong about spending the substantial amount of time that I do building relationship with the man whom I will spend the rest of my earthly life with!

The Devil is a liar and he indeed "comes to steal, kill, and destroy" (John 10:10). He wants to cripple your thoughts and get you off the path of righteousness to instead lead you to "a path that seems right…but leads only to death" (Proverbs 14:12).

I urge you my brothers and sisters to not "grow weary in well doing" (2Thessalonians 3:13). There is absolutely nothing wrong with living a God-centered and God-focused life. In fact that's exactly what you should be doing, but if you're like me and you find yourself feeling a little stale every now and then, then feel free to spice it up! Stir it up! Change it up!

"Go to a restaurant you've never been to before, dye your hair, put on some makeup, cut your hair, go shopping, take a fun class, get salsa lessons, or take a weekend trip…." The list goes on and on; either way do something to get things going for you again.

Minister Lindsay told me that according to her Pastor Mike Freeman, "if you want something better, you have to do something different."

I have been so inspired now to really take a hold to that advice and just add a little splash of color to my life. I know that I can't expect for excitement to just show up on my door step, I have to go out and get it.

So take a second and first thank God for where He has you right now, "in all situations [learn] to be content" (Philippians 4:11), secondly, get off Facebook for a little while; stop researching the lives of others and start living yours, and lastly, dive in and discover what gets you excited and stir it up!

~Candace

Posted by Candace and Tommy at <u>11:21 AM</u>

-So true Candace.....I get the exact same thoughts also at times....and then Holy Spirit reminds me that I am and can only be me! I have to do ME and live out my life the best way I can! At times we get so consumed with the lives of others (thru things like FB) that we ignore our own lives. Doing something new to get something different is SO ABSOLUTELY key! God desires for us to live out life to the full! We just have to get creative and do it!!! Thanks for the reminder :-)

Write on your Heart: *Philippians 4:11*

_____

_____

_____

_____

_____

_____

_____

_____

_____

_____

_____

_____

_____

_____

_____

_____

_____

_____

_____

Tuesday, December 23, 2008

<u>"The Present"</u>

"Yesterday Is History, Tomorrow Is A Mystery, Today Is A Gift That's Why We Call It The Present." — Eleanor Roosevelt

Since it is the week of Christmas I thought it would be fitting to write something about "Gifts" the book of Proverbs says: "Do not boast about tomorrow for we do not know what a day may bring forth". On the contrary, Paul said: "He forgets what was behind him and strains toward what's ahead". So if we shouldn't concern ourselves about tomorrow and yet we shouldn't look backwards, what should we do? I guess we should focus on today. Today, I asked Candace if she was enjoying the season of our Engagement and she said, "Yes!" I'm glad because I think that's all we need to worry about for now. Our future Forecast marriage and our past showcased dating which in reality neither means too much right now. So, today Candace and I are engaged and I guess we don't just need to focus on stirring "it" up But Stirring up our "Gift" of Today in particular.

What has God blessed us with right now that we need to focus on stirring up? My friend who is married gave me some great advice and encouragement about why waiting to get married before having sex is so key he said, "It's the only time that we get to build these spiritual and physical muscles" and after hearing that it just made sense I don't want to wait until marriage to learn how to listen/communicate to my wife or wait to learn how to give love and affection without wanting something in return. Can it be learned in marriage? Yes, of course but why wait? Have you ever tried to study for a test after the teacher passed it out? I have, and it doesn't work very well. Better yet if you're an athlete have you ever tried to workout or train after the game has started? I haven't but I would love to play against an opponent that did. What are we doing for our OFF SEASON and ON-SEASON workouts? How are we preparing for our test to come? We should be getting ready, developing that character, kindness, patience, and gentleness. Get ready now! Whether if we are single, dating, engaged, or married we shouldn't be worried about our past nor future, we should be concerned about our "Gift" called the PRESENT.

Merry Christmas! Enjoy your Gift!

~ Tommy

Posted by Candace and Tommy at <u>9:04 PM</u>

-SO key!!! I have made it a point to maximize the present season I am in at this point in life. It is only then that I will be adequately prepared for the next season. Great blog you guys!!

Write on your Heart: *Proverbs 27:1*

_____

_____

_____

_____

_____

_____

_____

_____

_____

_____

_____

_____

_____

_____

_____

_____

_____

_____

_____

Sunday, January 11, 2009

<u>"Taking Care of Business"</u>

Wow, where do I begin… So much has transpired since our last blog. I could share with you my experience of being a supportive fiancé and friend to Tommy during the passing of his last grandparent, or how stressful the financial portion of planning a wedding can be, or even how testing it is sometimes to learn the importance of really work as one, or most recently the pressing attention needed to have clear communication with one another. But instead I have decided to share with you my gratitude to have Tommy as my friend and soon-to-be husband. Ladies, there is nothing more appealing to me right now than his astounding humility and intentional love for me!

I am seriously in awe of how humble he is; now often times when we argue it's because of something that I messed up on (and no, right or wrong should never be the focus of a disagreement), but who likes to be wrong? Anyway, growing in Christ with Tommy has really taught me how to live in excellence and in love. He's not too proud to admit or to apologize when he makes a mistake or realizes he didn't respond in love. That blows my mind; the Bible says that … "Husbands are to treat their wives like Christ treats the church…" and Tommy is truly an example of that word.

It is my advice to you to always speak up and tell those around you and especially your partner of your admiration for them. And as humble as they may be, it's always encouraging to know that you appreciate and notice their effort in loving you. After listening to a sermon by Pastor Bryan E. Crute and Lynette Crute of Destiny Metropolitan Church in Atlanta, GA, I learned the importance of respect and admiration towards your husband. This word really touched me; it reminded me that nothing is ever too small to celebrate and your man is probably just praying and wishing you notice his effort to love you.

Don't be like the wife in T.D. Jake's new film "Not Easily Broken"; don't ignore and push your man so far away that he finds the need to look for love and respect outside your marriage. Ask yourself, "Who's taking care of my man?"

I know I am!!! And I pray and declare that no one else will ever have to answer that question for me.

~ Candace

Posted by Candace and Tommy at 6:38 PM 1 comments

-Two young Christians...in love...doing it right...and teaching others...WITHOUT BEING BORING!!! Yes god!!!

Write on your Heart: *1 Corinthians: 13:4-7*

Wednesday, January 28, 2009

"A Woman without her Man is nothing"

Depending on your own experiences or even how you view me will probably determine how you interpret or think about this title.

This weekend while Candace and I were out in D.C. an older lady came up to us after seeing that we were engaged and said " See I think every man has a rib out there somewhere and when you two walked into the room I could tell you two were together." Then she proceeded after many other words to say, "And Young Man I think you found your rib!"

It is so unique and amazing to me how Christ took the Rib out of the Man to create the Woman, and then births Men out of Women to create this complete circle of life. Therefore, he made us so relational that we need both of us, male and female in order to exist; we are compliments of one another. I'm sure there is a reason why Candace can hold a conversation longer than I can, and there is a reason I think big picture while Candace thinks details; it is needed for us to reach a level of fullness together.

Our Pastor Donnell Jones (Not the singer) put it best to us one day: "The Bible says in a marriage two become "one" not the same." Therefore, just like a Nut and a Bolt are two separate individual items, but when put together they make perfect unity. So are a Husband and Wife. You may be asking "How does this all tie back into Sexual Purity?" Well by not giving yourself away before you are married and have made a total commitment to each other, it forces you to not only begin to acknowledge each others' differences but it also opens up the door for you to be able to appreciate each others' differences. So for us as individuals, we need to work on our qualities that we will bring to the circle so we can help fulfill our mate. For couples, we should try to focus on what our mate contributes to our fulfillment. Our God is such a relational God and I truly believe he puts people in our lives so we can get extra glimpses of who He really is. So as Candace and I move towards our oneness, all I can say is:

"A Woman: without her, Man is Nothing." Or
"A Woman without her Man, is nothing."
I think both of them fit, you pick.

~ Tommy

Posted by Candace and Tommy at <u>12:21 PM</u>

-Great blog brother!! It all comes full circle with those last two sentences.

-You had me at, "Christ took the Rib out of the Man to create the Woman, and then births Men out of Women to create this complete circle of life." That is amazing. I guess I always knew it worked, but thinking about the logic of why God designed it that way...that's a whole different revelation!

Thanks for sharing.

Write on your Heart: *Genesis 2:23-24*

Tuesday, February 3, 2009

<u>Time</u>

Don't be discouraged by the interruptions in your time and planning. As frustrating and annoying as it can be, see them as opportunities for your growth and submission to God. I share this with you out of my personal challenges and tests of surrendering "my time" to God. When my plans are interrupted or just totally thrown out the window, I'm reminded that I am directed by God and His timing is best. For me, I am beginning to enjoy and accept Tommy as God's provision for my need for companionship.

I think everyone needs that one person who is like your cheerleader and a source of encouragement, especially during the times of frustration when you feel like your plans have been totally discarded. My fiancé really fulfills that need for companionship and support. God knows "exactly what you need even before you ask" (Matthew 6:32) so not only should you trust God when your life is "interrupted," but also learn to enjoy and receive your spouse as God's perfect provision for your needs , especially during those times.

~Candace

Write on your Heart: *Matthew 7:25-32*

_____

_____

_____

_____

_____

_____

_____

_____

_____

_____

_____

_____

_____

_____

_____

_____

_____

_____

_____

Tuesday, February 10, 2009

<u>Network!!!</u>

Ohhh My!! Ohhh My!! 2009 is getting real. What a Great year it has been thus far, we've gained a New President, The Pittsburgh Steelers just won the Super bowl!!, and I'm getting married in a little over 5 Months I mean it's getting real if it hasn't already. For Candace and myself, wedding planning is going great everything seems to be in order, payments are being made, invitations are going out; this wedding stuff is going as smooth as possible. We can give a tremendous amount of credit to Candace's SISTERS, our families; and a host of friends for helping us with this. It is so comforting to be covered and surrounded with so much Love and prayer. No matter what phase we are at in life it is a must that our network consist of a host of people that will encourage, uplift, and strengthen us with truthful words that we need to hear. Not words that we want to hear but words that we need to hear. I'm more than grateful that we have that. To keep this blog short and sweet, I Corinthians 15:33 says "Bad Company corrupts Good Character" If we want to make this year as great as it possibly can be, we all need to stay away from "Bad Company" and instead surround ourselves with people that will give us Prophetic words not Pathetic words. We are still about saving lives now! We must remember to be supported with Good Character before we try to save Bad Company. My Network is way better than Verizon. Who's in your Network? WRITE IT DOWN FOR YOURSELF!

~ Tommy

Posted by Candace and Tommy at <u>8:12 PM</u>

-Right on!

-Thanks for the shout out Bro. Ya'll have a great Network, not only because I am in it, but because the one up above it. And unlike Sprint, he never drops calls!

Write on your Heart: *I Corinthians 15:33*

_____

_____

_____

_____

_____

_____

_____

_____

_____

_____

_____

_____

_____

_____

_____

_____

_____

_____

_____

_____

Sunday, February 22, 2009

<u>Sexual Tension: Re-directed</u>

Hi, hope ya'll have been blessed by the stories and thoughts Tommy and I share so openly with you; it's been almost 7 months since our first blog and I'm so flabbergasted by all that God has done in our lives and the lives of you all, the blog readers. I pray that God will continue to inspire us and use us to bless your lives.

So with that said, I want to share with ya'll the consistent reminder that I have been receiving from sources that will go unnamed… of the importance of really spending time in God's presence daily. Now before I go on, let me preface this by saying that this is not a "quick-fix" or a "get out of temptation free" tool, but rather just the will of God for our and your lives.

Alright, so the other day I realized that Tommy and I had been really "good" if you would, as it pertains to our sexual purity; my thought –life was pure, we overall or at least I didn't experience any recent sexual urges or temptations.. To God be the Glory. But when I began praising God for that, especially thinking about how close we are to being married and how difficult it can be to really "run from sexual sin" (1 Corinthians 6:18) and to live " holy" (1 Thessalonians 4:3), I said "wow, God this is really great!"

I thought about if there was anything we did that was different than in the months past: had we not been spending that much time together? But that wasn't the case; the truth of the matter is that we had both been consistently and faithfully seeking God's face. God exchanged and redirected our sexual tension with His Attention. And as not to boast in ourselves, because it's the Holy Spirit that draws you to the Lord (1 Corinthians 12:3), but our thoughts and actions were so on Christ, that we did not make time for distractions.

Now yes, of course distractions came and I'm sure will continue to come right up until we say "I Do", but honestly staying fed by God and exercising it with others: believers in Christ and non-believers helped to keep us in right-standing with God.

So, I hope that was helpful to many of you who may be struggling in this area, but for those of you who have had success with this, we'd love to get your feedback of this question:

Q: How do you allow God to participate in the sexual tension re-routing and re-directing process in your daily lives?

~ Candace

Posted by Candace and Tommy at <u>6:21 PM</u>

-"God exchanged and redirected our sexual tension with His Attention. And as not to boast in ourselves, because it's the Holy Spirit that draws you to the Lord (1 Corinthians 12:3), but our thoughts and actions were so on Christ, that we did not make time for distractions." I think this is so key and is very important to take note of. I have found that when I keep my eyes, attention, energy, emotions, etc.

focused on Christ, distraction has a difficult time getting into my system. God keeps me occupied when I LET Him. Not that I am always physically dong something, but He keeps my mind constantly on Him...day in and day out... It's amazing!

-Great Blog....

Write on your Heart:
* *I Corinthians 6:18*
* *Psalm: 119:9*

_____

_____

_____

_____

_____

_____

_____

_____

_____

_____

_____

_____

_____

_____

_____

_____

_____

_____

Tuesday, March 3, 2009

<u>Tunes from the Heart</u>

A few days ago, someone had the audacity to ask me if Candace and I ever got into arguments or got into disputes. My answer was, "What? Do we? Man, we be going at it much more than either one of us like," If you know me then you know that I'm a let you know how I feel type person right out the gate; I'm pretty much what you see is what you get, and Candace is no slouch in that area either. Therefore, sometimes those two personality traits clash. Yet, I can honestly say that the disputes that we get into are healthy arguments/disagreements that need to be settled. They usually start off with very small offenses that don't get acknowledged or stated up front that ends up growing into a big conflict. For instance, this past weekend Candace was starting to tell me how she thought one event reminded her of another event when I jumped right in and told her how I begged to differ before she even got to finish her statement. Of course, she was offended but instead of me seizing the opportunity to APOLOGIZE I held to my statement and the conflict escalated from there. Then, after a long drawn out sequence of dramatic conversations we got back to the main issue and cleared everything up. So that was my example of being quick to speak and slow to listen. (I learned it doesn't turnout very well.) I guess that's why the Good Book says (James 1:19) "be quick to listen, slow to speak and slow to get angry". Not just listening to the person's words but to their "Heart" behind the words. Be quick to listen to the "Heart". As we all seize this opportunity of purity we gain a more sensitive ear to the Heart. Are you Sensitive to the Tunes from the Heart?

~ Tommy

Posted by Candace and Tommy at <u>6:16 PM</u>

-Wow! I have being reading over you all post, and this is great! My 14 year old cousin has recently said she wants to join this great revolution of it's worth the wait or courtship! I am so glad that you all have decided to blog about your journey and be a living example for young girls like her! I look forward to reading more and discussing your journey with her and keeping her accountable. Thanks

Write on your Heart: *James 1:19*

_____

_____

_____

_____

_____

_____

_____

_____

_____

_____

_____

_____

_____

_____

_____

_____

_____

_____

Monday, March 9, 2009

<u>"Learning how to be loved"</u>

This weekend Tommy and I along with his mother visited my family in beautiful Atlanta, GA. It was a fabulous time of fun, excitement, laughter, and love. I couldn't have asked for a better time of unity. And as I sat in amazement of how awesome and detailed God is, I realized how loved I am by my family and by Tommy as well.

With wedding planning all ready and finalized I found myself getting a little too needy and sometimes just plain out wanting too much. Learning how to be loved takes a certain level of humility and that's what I experienced this weekend. I'm fortunate enough to have wonderfully talented sisters and mother that our wedding was practically custom-made for Tommy and I.

Now there's a difference between being controlled and being loved; and I'm glad to say that I experience the latter. When someone offers to help you and to do something for you, don't let pride stop your blessing. We are never too "grown" or too particular to accept someone else's help and suggestion.

This also does not mean to take advantage of other's giving; be lead by the Holy Spirit and return to those that which they deserve. When someone decides to pour into your life they are sowing seed with the intent and prayer that it will yield good fruit. So be grateful for the love you receive, use it to produce good fruit and simply enjoy being loved.

Not accepting love is just as prideful as thinking that you deserve it and that it's your right to receive it.

Receive God's gift of love (1 John 4:16), and as you are lead by the Spirit receive those whom He uses to love you in the natural also.

Sometimes you just have to learn how to be loved!!

~Candace

Posted by Candace and Tommy at <u>6:56 PM</u>

Write on your Heart: *1 John 4:16*

Wednesday, March 18, 2009

<u>Blessed to be a Blessing</u>

I'm a firm believer that we as a people are blessed to be a blessing. It is so easy to get so consumed with one's self and think that everything that we receive is for us, but I totally beg to differ. I can't even count the amount of people/couples that have poured into our lives and blessed us and everyday I pray that we will do the same to others. We never know who is watching us and we never know what effects our relationship or actions will have on other people; we can either leave a really bitter taste with someone or a great taste. I hope we leave the latter. The more Candace and I try to strengthen our Christian walk with purity and holiness the more we realize that this really isn't just about us but it's about everyone we come into contact with and the generations that will follow us that are trying to build a relationship with Jesus. As we stated at the beginning of this blog to everyone that is being faithful to Christ and is part of this "Worth the Wait Revolution," Wait doesn't necessarily mean forever. According to our wedding website Candace and I have 123 days left and we can't wait...I mean we will wait...Ahh you know what I mean.... But seriously, we as believers are called to be the salt of the world (Matthew 5:13) and one of Salt's uses is to reduce bitterness. When we come in contact with others by us being the salt we have the opportunity of leaving others feeling bitter or assisting them to feel better... Do you leave people feeling/ tasting Bitter or Better?

`Tommy

Posted by Candace and Tommy at <u>2:22 AM</u>

-I love your blogs!!! I'm so glad that you guys have been consistent with it and are providing content through your testimonies. You are truly an inspiring and amazing couple!!! I know you will live a fulfilled life full of abundance.

-Hi there Candace I read your comment that you left on superswagger I hope all is well. Jesus is the best thing that has happened to all of us who've received him he brought us with his own blood. My life your life is not our own. All that we do must glorify him and the Father. There is no such thing as doing our thing we believers do the word and live the word. People can't see God but they see the ones who represent him People are dying and going to hell everyday. The world needs us as believers to be who we are and not like them. They are hungry for a way out they need to see a difference they need to see Gods love.

God Bless

-Great Blog. Love it. Very inspirational.

Write on your Heart: *Genesis 12:2-3 * Matthew 5:13*

_____

_____

_____

_____

_____

_____

_____

_____

_____

_____

_____

_____

_____

_____

_____

_____

_____

_____

_____

_____

Thursday, March 26, 2009

"What a Man wants, What a Man needs"

Ladies, I thought I knew, but I had no idea. There is something that the men in our lives need more than love, money, or even sex! It's RESPECT!!!

I learned this a while back, but over the past few weeks I saw it play out much differently than I had imagined. I thought respect for my fiancé was telling him how proud I am of him, and how much I love him, and how excited I am to have him be the leader of our household. When little did I know I wasn't giving him the respect he truly needed.

According to our marriage counselors, my fiancé, like most men, didn't need an "A- da boy; great job", he needed me to trust him, trust his abilities, his judgments, and most of all trust the God in him.

Respect for him is a silent, quiet, respect that speaks louder than words. It's the stillness of my lips when he makes a "wrong" turn, but I just wait patiently trusting that he knows where he's going and that we'll get there on time, and it's even the bigger things like trusting that he knows we're getting married in just as little as 4 months and that he's setting himself up, with Christ's help, to be able to provide for our family and give me the security that like most women, I need.

The RESPECT factor is huge to any man, whether it is your significant other, father, uncle, pastor, mentor, or brother.

The Men in our lives want to know that we really trust them and even more so, that we trust their relationship with Christ.

So, I share this with you because this personally is a challenge for me; I am very verbal and opinionated, and although I do trust and respect my fiancé, I sometimes talk entirely way too much or just at the wrong time.

These are just a few verses that help me to remember how to respect my fiancé:

Ephesians 5: 33 "So again I say, each man must love his wife as he loves himself, and the wife must RESPECT her husband." (New Living Translation)

Proverbs 13:3 "Those who control their tongue will have a long life; opening your mouth can ruin everything." (New Living Translation)

Proverbs 10:19 "Too much talk leads to sin. Be sensible and keep your mouth shut." (New Living Translation)

~Candace

Posted by Candace and Tommy at 3:24 PM

-Great Post Candace! It really is wonderful to see what God is teaching you, and through you. Thank you to you and Tommy for this blog, as I find it to be a fantastic refresher during the actual practical everyday life of marriage with kids! Love you!

Write on your Heart: Proverbs 10:19

_____

_____

_____

_____

_____

_____

_____

_____

_____

_____

_____

_____

_____

_____

_____

_____

_____

_____

Sunday, April 5, 2009

<u>He Lives in You</u>

We are elated and thankful when people tell us this blog is inspirational; but one thing we want to set straight is that this blog is not meant to be inspirational but rather made to be educational. My view of inspirational is when you look at something and have the response of Wow! What they are doing is great. On the contrary, things that are educational not only have you saying wow! What they are doing is great, but I feel empowered & equipped to do the same thing. Our motivation for this blog is not just to share what Candace and I are learning on our journey towards marriage. Instead our motivation to show you what Christ has done in our lives and is capable of doing in yours. If you know Candace or myself then you know that neither one of us has a spotless past, that is until we allowed the Holy spirit to rest inside us to cleanse and forgive us of our past, present, and future. Furthermore, the Holy Spirit has defined us and I can think of no better example than this:

Most of my close friends know that the Lion King is one of my favorite movies; I think it is so much deeper than animation. Specifically I want to concentrate on the part where Simba forgets who he is; and the Baboon (Rafiki) has to remind him of not only who he is but more importantly who he comes from. He comes from MUFASA the KING of PRIDE ROCK! Therefore, that is really what this blog is about, a reminder of who we come from the real KING the real ROCK (JESUS CHRIST). It is totally understood that this world has the ability to make us sometimes forget like

Simba. Also, like Simba I think it's our duty to look deep into our reflection. If we don't see anything at first I think we need to take Rafiki's advice and "LOOK HARDER". Until we are fully convinced that he lives in me and he lives in you (Gen 1:26-29) and understand we are called to be Kings and Queens since we are made in his Image. In conclusion, I would like to restate we are so thankful for your encouraging words, but this blog is so not about us; it's more so about the Christ that lives in us. By which empowers us to live this lifestyle of sexual purity. Finally, I have a strong conviction that it is no accident that you're reading this blog. It is meant for you, Yes you! To realize that "He Lives in you".

~Tommy

Posted by Candace and Tommy at 9:26 PM

-I feel that to inspire means to motivate others to do better. The fact that you guys share your testimonies and seem to be consistent not only in what you say be also what you do inspires others to want to do the same thing. You are an inspiration because it allows others to see, though we know we have our savior, the testimony of others to know that "no, we are not doing this on our own."

-I'm just happy that you are continuing your blog and updating it frequently. It gives my boyfriend and me encouragement when the flesh is week: mentally, physically or spiritually, even though we pray and read the bible often. Remember that though people are educated doesn't mean that they practice what they are taught, but to inspire is to influence thought or practice thus helping to change people and their relationships with GOD others. Just think of Howard or Church... The teachers and preachers that you look up to didn't just educate you but they made you want to use what you learned to make yourself and the "Global Community" better. So you are doing your job of educating... But don't be afraid of inspiring, encouraging and motivating others to be more like Christ. Keep being consistent.

Write on your Heart: *Genesis 1:26-29*

_____

_____

_____

_____

_____

_____

_____

_____

_____

_____

_____

_____

_____

_____

_____

_____

_____

_____

_____

_____

Tuesday, April 14, 2009

<u>Influential Woman:</u>

Over the past few weeks I have been realizing how critical of a role my attitude plays in altering the environment of our relationship. Tommy detests a negative/or complaining spirit and for him any kind of complaint without a solution is futile and utterly destructive for a person's spirit. (Remember, these are my words not his…but from what I gather from our conversations and his response to complaining attitudes, this is the bottom line.)

And truthfully, I agree with him, although sometimes you just want to vent about your day or just your frustrations. I used to think, "yeah, that's the great part about having a mate: someone to talk to about EVERYTHING, someone to just be truthful and transparent with. But the reality is, no matter how open and transparent your relationship is; your man is not your girlfriend, and most of all he is not God! He has bad days too, and you have to be sensitive to when is right time to vent or simply "express your feelings" and when you should just leave your frustrations at the Father's feet, and have a quiet and content spirit.

This can be a challenge for me, but as I continue to grow in Christ and also learn my role as a woman, and as a wife-to-be, I am beginning to grasp the concept of truly "Seeking first the Kingdom of Heaven". You see, if I continue to "VENT, AND VENT, AND VENT" Tommy begins to get worn out and "un-motivated" to talk to me. There is only so much negative talk you can share; you have to use wisdom and realize the power and influence that you as a woman truly have in setting the environment for your male/female relationships.

So as I practice these tools myself, I encourage you ladies to also apply the skill of applying the 5 W's a little differently:

1. Knowing WHO to talk to

2. WHAT to share with them

3. WHERE is the best place to talk

4. WHEN is the right time to bring up the subject

5. WHY you're choosing to share this issue/subject with them.

***Remember, despite how strong, protective, wise, or patient your Superman is, he is still just a man, a mere human, and Truthfully, God should be the 1st one you run to when you're overwhelmed or stressed, or confused, or whatever! Seeking Christ first will allow you to do all your talking and expressing without talking his ear off, and it will also allow the Holy Spirit to enter your situation and calm you down. And lastly, you will hopefully have received a new direction or solution to your issue that you can positively share with your man.

Most men are problem solvers, so talking just to talk can get really old and frustrating for them, but if you already have a solution, they may be a little more inclined to engage in the conversation, knowing there's a point to the story, and better yet, that you're positively responding to it.

Well I hope this was helpful, I'd love to know your thoughts on the issue.

~Candace

Posted by Candace and Tommy at <u>6:57 AM</u>

Write on your Heart: *Philippians 4:8-9*

_____

_____

_____

_____

_____

_____

_____

_____

_____

_____

_____

_____

_____

_____

_____

_____

_____

_____

_____

Sunday, April 26, 2009

What is inside of you?

Wow! We are actually down to less than 85 days until our wedding day. On our strive to oneness we are actually having to make real decisions along the process. For instance, how are we paying for the wedding, where are we going to live, how we are going to handle our finances, etc? As we make these serious decisions we really are getting a heavy dose of true intimacy. Like our Pastor's wife constantly states, "Intimacy means just that, (In- to me –u – See)" being in a relationship and actually having to discuss real issues can really bring the realness out of each other. Now, making these small decisions although they seem big to us gives us the opportunity to see what actually makes us tick, and exposes what is actually inside of us. The more Candace and I try to implement the characteristics of Christ in our lives the better we are at interacting together. The Holy Spirit guides us to respond accordingly over and over again. We can only respond consistently with a gentle answer to turn away from conflict/destruction if the Holy Spirit rest within us. Which brings me to my main point on why we need to flee from Sexual immorality (1 Corinthians 6:18) because where Lust, Selfishness, perversion, and the like rest, the Holy Spirit will refuse to rest! The Holy Spirit is all about Love, Giving, and Purity. What's inside of you?

~Tommy

Posted by Candace and Tommy at 7:37 PM

81

Re-Write on your Heart: *1 Corinthians 6:18*

_____

_____

_____

_____

_____

_____

_____

_____

_____

_____

_____

_____

_____

_____

_____

_____

_____

_____

_____

Tuesday, May 19, 2009

<u>"I like you"</u>

Hi, I can't believe our wedding is less than 59 days away. It is absolutely amazing to see the transformation God has done in us over the last 2 + years. I don't think it's actually hit me yet that I'll have the marvelous responsibility of being a wife, and some day mother, but this week I want to share with you some of the things God has revealed to me throughout our courtship.

During this 2+ years, I have grown to understand a little bit more about how selfish I can be at times, and truth be told, I don't think you know how selfish you really are until you have to share with someone else. Tommy has learned the importance of how to speak truth in love, and how to express his love for me in a way that I can receive it, whether that be through affirmation or a hug. And truly, the list goes on. And I'm sure we will continue to grow, shed layers, and be molded by God into the best woman/wife/mother, and man/husband/father He wants us to be in the coming years of marriage.

Another thing that I have realized lately is just how much fun I have with Tommy. We have these really crazy laughing spells sometimes that we just can't control. I mean, if there's one thing I love to do, it's to laugh! And what a pleasure it is to be able to experience such joy with your friend and soon-to-be spouse. Now as ya'll know from our previous blog entries, it's not always laughs, but as the book of Ecclesiastes says, there is a time for everything, and I'm glad we get to experience both sadness and laughter. I appreciate so much more the times when we are in our "Happy Place" as our marriage counselors call it.

In addition God has reminded me just how nice of a person Tommy is and how fortunate I am to have him as a friend and a future husband. I mean, one day we were on the phone together and I just had this Ah-ha moment of, "wow, you're just so nice, I just like you….I mean you're fun, and just so nice. " LOL and for those of you who know Tommy personally you know he's a man of few words and replied, "…thanks…?"

Well, to wrap it up, I just want to say thanks for traveling with us through our journey and I can't wait to share more with ya'll as we near the big day. And if there's one thing to take away from this entry, it's to take some time and just think about where you're at in life and where you were just a few months or years ago, and how different things are (hopefully). God can really do some great things in your life if you just allow Him to be Sovereign and lead you; now you do have to put in your part, but don't ever forget who the true director in this story of life is.

Love ya'll,   ~Candace soon-to-be Claiborn IV

Posted by Candace and Tommy at 7:38 PM

-Daughter of mine and future son on mine, you are fearfully and wonderfully made. It makes me extremely proud to see how quickly God is maturing you both. It is a pleasure to witness the two becoming one already in spirit and truth.

Love mom

Write on your Heart: *Ecclesiastes 3:4*

_____

_____

_____

_____

_____

_____

_____

_____

_____

_____

_____

_____

_____

_____

_____

_____

_____

_____

_____

_____

Tuesday, May 26, 2009

<u>Who's The Bride?</u>

In Ephesians 5:31-33 Paul states to the Ephesians church, " For this reason a man will leave his father and mother and be united to his wife and the two will become one flesh: This is a profound mystery but I am talking about Christ and the Church. However each one of you also must love his wife as he loves himself and the wife must respect her husband."

Every time I read that passage I'm amazed by Paul's wisdom. Also, every time I read this verse I'm encouraged to become better. (A better man, a better fiancé', & soon to be better husband.) The more I understand that I'm a part of the church (Christ's Bride) and I see how he treats his bride (me) the standard I set for myself rises that much higher on how I should treat my Bride. To his Bride he's always gentle, compassionate, patient, humble, encouraging, and forgiving; he makes his bride pure. That's the kind of Husband I inspire to be like, I want to be like Christ. I want to treat my Bride the way that Christ treats us; I believe anything else is missing the mark. Although, I know it's easier said than done I'm willing to try. Every time I'm offended by Candace I begin to hear a small voice in my head that says, "Why or how does she do that to me?" But not even a split moment later I also get a conviction in my Heart from the Holy Spirit that states, "Why and how do you do that to me?" Instantly I know I must forgive her and Love her with all my heart. Even though, I still don't respond as speedy and prompt as I should, this is where I'm growing at in life.

"Although I'm nowhere close to where I need to be. I strive to treat my Bride to be, the same way Christ treats the bride in me."

How do you want to be like Christ? WRITE IT DOWN! And ACT ON IT

~Tommy

Posted by Candace and Tommy at <u>10:28 AM</u>

Write on your Heart: *Ephesians 5:31-33*

Wednesday, June 3, 2009

<u>Six tips for being Six weeks out</u>

The events leading up to the wedding can be so much fun; this weekend I had my first bridal shower , next weekend will be the Atlanta bridal shower, Tommy and I will sign the lease to our first apartment, and then before we know it we'll be back in Atlanta for our wedding!

As things begin to speed up, I have created a reminder list for myself on how to stay focused over the next six weeks before our wedding. Like any big experience, you know that there is often a calming before the storm and you must guard yourself and your heart so as to not be distracted. After all, "the enemy comes to steal, kill, and destroy."

Here are my top 6 tips for being 6 weeks out:

1. Remain Accountable: Stay covered and grounded; these are the weeks when you're waiting season seems so close to its end, and you have to continue to remind and encourage yourself that "your fruit will bear in due season" (Psalms 1:3) Sometimes I get so excited and anxious about our marriage, that I forget to simply enjoy the season that we are currently in. We have to tighten our belts and use wisdom in how we spend our time together.

2. Remain in a disciple relationship: My mom and I have been reading Stormie Omartian's book, "The Power of a Praying Wife." This has been a great opportunity for

my mom and I to both grow and also for her to pour into me as I transition into a new phase of womanhood (as corny as that may sound). It's been a great read and helps me to prepare. I know that there are only so many books and studies that you can take part in, and that the real experience comes from just experiencing marriage, but use the resources around you to at least build up some reserves.

3. Have fun!!!! Enjoy the showers and the gifts, and the time "being single." Not that, marriage puts you in some type of crazy bondage, but just enjoy the season of being single!

4. Stay prayed up! Continue to fill yourself with the Word of God. God's word and the Holy Spirit is really what is carrying me at this point. It's been easy for me to get distracted by the stresses of work and the attractive lingerie. Lol I have to stay in the word of God. Now I'm not really a morning person, and there are different views on when is a good time to seek God, but really yes you can seek Him anytime and you should seek Him all throughout the day, but giving Him your attention first thing in the morning, I believe will help to keep you covered and focused before you even step out into the world of chaos. I didn't really get this concept until I tried it, and it made all the difference in how I started my day.

5. Love your fiancé, but don't get too lovely –dovey with him. Ladies, yes he is a Christian, but he is also a man, and you can be sure that his hormones are raging and ready to really "minister" to you! So just be conscious of the subtle things you may do, say, or wear, that can

possibly trigger something in your man. And of course it's different for everyone, you just have to study and learn your partner.

6. Tie up any loose financial ends: make sure you are both clear on how you will be stewards of your money both for your lives as a married couple and also for the remaining wedding and housing expenses. Communication is really the key in this area. Don't purchase or make any financial decisions without consulting your fiancé especially if it affects you both. This is not just, "oh why do I have to get permission?" it's simply out of respect and a form of protection for you. Shoot, if you haven't gotten the idea that it's not just about you anymore and that you need to communicate your choices, and then the next 6 weeks is a great time to get that revelation.

Love ya'll; talk to you during week 4. ~ Candace

Posted by Candace and Tommy at 10:37 AM

Write on your Heart: *Psalm 1:3*

Thursday, June 11, 2009

<u>"Prayer Changes Things"</u>

36 days until "THE BIG DAY" Through pre-marital counseling one of the many great things we learned was how to pray with each other. All of our counselors recommended that we pray together at least once a week if not more. Candace and I haven't been as consistent as we would like at this and it reflects in our relationship and how we interact with others. Our marriage prep counselors taught us a 3 part prayer to do in 6 minutes 3:6. 3 different parts 1 minute each (because ya'll know how some people be trying to pray forever.)

Part 1 is about the things we are THANKFUL for; Part 2 are the areas we need to REPENT in and Part 3 we PRAY FOR OUR SIGNIFICANT OTHERS. Strong, Quick, and Powerful all one minute each, 3 parts. 3:6. this morning Candace and I took the initiative to make sure we did and I'm very grateful for that because it revealed a lot to me. First, it showed me that it gives us the ability to affirm each other on a consistent basis. Next, I noticed it reveals to us the areas that we know that we messed up in so the other doesn't have to go out of our way to try to point out that area. We can have faith that GOD is working it out. Then, it gives us the opportunity to encourage and uplift one another in areas that we need it. Finally, and most importantly it keeps GOD in the center of our relationship. With 36 days left until we are officially "ONE" we are trying to implement 3:6 into our relationship on a more consistent basis. Feel free to hold us accountable. "Prayer Changes things."

~Tommy

Write on your Heart: *Matthew 6:9-15*

Oct, 16 2009

<u>BREAKTHROUGH!!!</u>

Well, our last blog was 36 days before our wedding, and needless to say we got Married on JULY 18, 2009 and that night we got ENDORSED by Dr. Lindsay Marsh, President and CEO of "WORTH THE WAIT", and more importantly we were endorsed by GOD in our covenant of marriage. On July 19, 2009 approximately 1:07 a.m. we umm… read our first book as a married couple and then we went ALL THE WAY….. To the Dominican Republic, Punta Cana and we read a lot of books…

Ok we had Sex and lots of it! Praise God for Waiting! Just for the record Dr. Marsh was right; it was the "Best Sex of our Lives". If anyone has any doubts about whether or not that 32 yr old Virgin knew what she was talking about let them doubt no more. We are here to stand and tell you that she is in tune with the Holy Spirit.

Our wedding turned out better than we could have imagined or prayed; the weather was beautiful, the set up was gorgeous, and most of all we could really sense the presence of the Lord. Neither of us had any qualms or doubts about our commitment to one another. Truthfully, it felt like our pastor was speaking sooooo slowly because we were so excited and ready to just be married already!!!

So we thought it would be fun to share some tips for the big day:

For the Bride:

1. Stay Prayed up!!!!! And get plenty of sleep the night before.

2. Don't let anyone or anything distract or upset you; the last thing you want to do is ruin your makeup, or miss out on all the fun you could be having with your girls.

3. Soak it up!!!! This is a GREAT DAY, and it only comes once (well for me at least). Take personal pictures if you can to keep memories of the behind the scenes moments.

4. Eat something; yes you'll be so anxious that you may not even think to eat, but at least eat a good breakfast to get you through the day.

5. Remember it's about you and your husband; he and Christ are the only ones you need to be concerned about. You're getting Married, and at the end of the day that's what it's all about, not the cake, what happened last night at the rehearsal dinner, if you know who might show up... and the list goes on.

P.S.**** Ladies if you have an outfit all picked out for your special night, don't be disappointed if you don't wear it until day 3 of the Honeymoon, your Husband is still pleased and I can almost promise you he won't be too distraught that he missed all the ribbons and bows to the best present of his married life! Lol

For the Groom:

1. Pray and Read your Bible; spend intimate time with God and give your day to him. Pray for your marriage and spouse-to-be.

2. Get a good breakfast.

3. Get your Bride a gift. Remember it is a day for the both of you but honestly it's her day.

4. Hang with your family, friends, and groomsmen to help keep you relaxed and grounded.

5. Be ready for distractions. Remember that the day is perfect no matter what as long as you, your bride, and pastor shows up. Most importantly remind yourself that it's just a day, but your marriage is for a lifetime.

*** Let your new form of Ministry begin….

All in all, we want everyone to B.L.O.G. their way to marriage. **B**reakthrough any generational curses on your life, **L**isten to the Holy Spirit intently, and **O**bey **G**od's commands. "You are Worth the Wait!!!" Hold the Line! Enjoy….